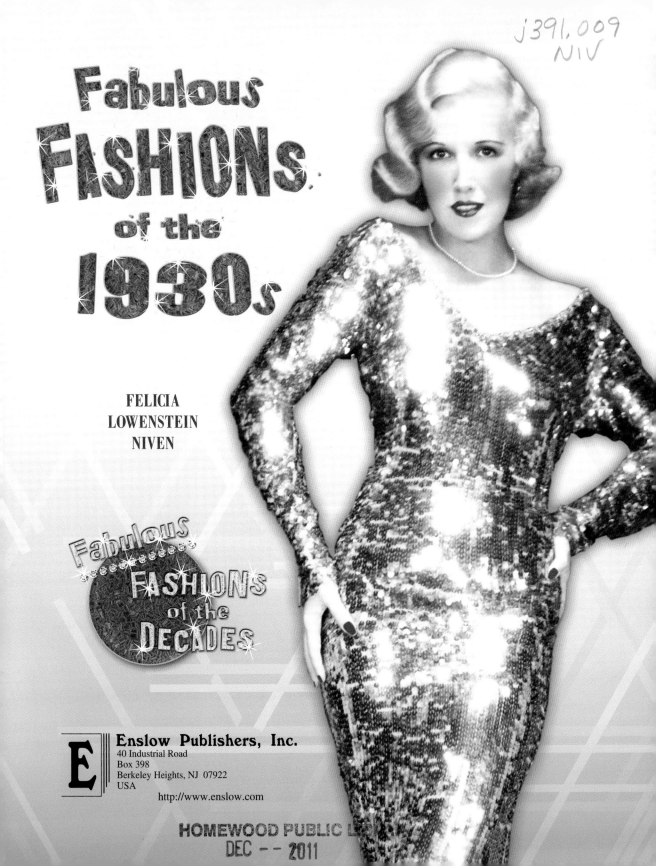

Fabulous FASHIONS of the 1930s

FELICIA LOWENSTEIN NIVEN

Fabulous FASHIONS of the DECADES

E **Enslow Publishers, Inc.**
40 Industrial Road
Box 398
Berkeley Heights, NJ 07922
USA

http://www.enslow.com

Library of Congress Cataloging-in-Publication Data

Niven, Felicia Lowenstein.
    Fabulous fashions of the 1930s / Felicia Lowenstein Niven.
       p. cm. — (Fabulous fashions of the decades)
    Fabulous fashions of the nineteen thirties
    Includes bibliographical references and index.
    Summary: "Discusses the fashions of the 1930s, including women's and men's clothing and hairstyles,
      accessories, trends and fads, and world events that influenced the fashion"—Provided by publisher.
    ISBN 978-0-7660-3824-0
      1. Fashion—History—20th century—Juvenile literature. 2. Fashion design—History—20th
century—Juvenile literature. 3. Lifestyle—History—20th century—Juvenile literature. 4. Nineteen
thirties—Juvenile literature. I. Title. II. Title: Fabulous fashions of the nineteen thirties.
    TT504.N565 2011
    746.9'2—dc22
                                2010014586

Paperback ISBN 978-1-59845-276-1

Printed in the United States of America

052011 Lake Book Manufacturing, Inc., Melrose Park, IL

10 9 8 7 6 5 4 3 2 1

To Our Readers: We have done our best to make sure all Internet Addresses in this book were active and appropriate when we went to press. However, the author and the publisher have no control over and assume no liability for the material available on those Internet sites or on other Web sites they may link to. Any comments or suggestions can be sent by e-mail to comments@enslow.com or to the address on the back cover.

Every effort has been made to locate all copyright holders of material used in this book. If any errors or omissions have occurred, corrections will be made in future editions of this book.

♻ Enslow Publishers, Inc., is committed to printing our books on recycled paper. The paper in every book contains 10% to 30% post-consumer waste (PCW). The cover board on the outside of each book contains 100% PCW. Our goal is to do our part to help young people and the environment too!

Illustration Credits: AP Images/Maurice Seymour, p. 19; © ClassicStock/Alamy, pp. 11, 18, 39; Dover Publications, Inc./Sears®, pp. 9, 14, 20, 22, 26, 30, 32, 37; Everett Collection, pp. 1, 12, 15, 41; The Granger Collection, NYC – All rights reserved., pp. 6, 21, 29, 34, 40; H. Armstrong Roberts/ClassicStock, p. 36; Hulton Archive/Getty Images, p. 24; Library of Congress, pp. 43–45; Rue des Archives/The Granger Collection, NYC – All rights reserved., p. 4; Shutterstock, p. 47; Time & Life Pictures/Getty Images, pp. 7, 28; © Underwood Photo Archives/SuperStock, p. 35.

Cover Illustration: Everett Collection (blonde in sequin gown).

Contents

The 1930s

The 1930s

Joan Crawford (1904–1977) exudes confidence and power in this asymmetrical number. The 1930s did away with the boyish look of the previous decade and once again welcomed feminine curves. Shoulder pads made women look curvier. Their waists appeared smaller because their shoulders were broader.

Wildest and Craziest Fads

Imagine being so poor that you had to stand in a bread-line for free food. You did not even have to be poor to be in need during the 1930s. This was the time of the Great Depression. Many people were out of work. It was one of the hardest times in our nation's history.

If you were worrying about food, you would not be spending money on fashion. You might "make do" with what you had in your closet.

Many women got really creative. In the 1930s, jewelry departments sold dress clips. They looked like large earrings. Women used them to change the look of a dress. If clipped along the top of the dress, it changed the neckline. The clips pulled it open and down to form a heart. This shape, later known as the sweetheart neckline, was popular fashion trend.

FABULOUS FASHIONS of the 1930s

Women also took note of what was worn in the movies. Going to the movies was an easy way to escape depressing daily life.

Actress Joan Crawford wore shoulder pads in the movie *Letty Lynton*. Shoulder pads also appeared in designs by Elsa Schiaparelli. Women added shoulder pads to dresses,

Katharine Hepburn (1907–2003) shows off heavily padded shoulders in this scene from the 1938 movie *Holiday*.

Italian fashion designer Elsa Schiaparelli (1890–1973) looks at a chart with samples of the fabrics used in her collection, January 1, 1938. She was influenced by surrealism, an art movement focusing on fantastical imagery. She experimented with Rhodophane, a thin, transparent fabric, in her designs. However, the strange material was more interesting to look at than practical to wear.

sweaters, and jackets. There were even reports of three-inch shoulder pads in nightgowns. Now that is a crazy fad!

Even fashions in historical movies were copied. If they could afford it, women wore the long velvet dresses and caps seen in *Romeo and Juliet*. They also wore the style of boater hat that Katharine Hepburn wore in *Little Women*.

FABULOUS FASHIONS of the 1930s

When Greta Garbo starred in *Mata Hari,* a romance based on the true-life story of the exotic spy, jeweled skullcaps became best-sellers. After she appeared in *The Painted Veil,* veiled pillbox hats were popular.

Science was also playing a role in fashion during the 1930s. This was a time when man-made materials were developed. Some, such as nylon, we still use today. Others were not so successful.

One fabric, called Rhodophane, looked like glass. It was made of cellophane and other man-made materials. It could appear like clear glass or a cobweb. Schiaparelli used Rhodophane in some dresses, purses, and shoes. But this glasslike fabric never caught on.

Chapter 1

Hairstyles

By the 1930s, women were tired of looking like boys. They added feminine touches to their hairstyles, such as waves, curls, and color. Styles were softer and fuller. Hats covered less of the head so the hair was in full view. That made hairstyles even more important.

Hair was mostly waved and chin or shoulder length during this time period. Supershort cuts were no longer the rage. Some women would even be able to pin their hair up into a chignon or bun.

Finger waves and pin curls could be done at home. Permanent waves were mostly done at salons. Bleaching or tinting could be done at either place. Either way, women ended up spending a lot of time, and money, on their hair during the 1930s.

Wave and Curl

Two popular styles could be done right at home: finger waves and pin curls. Finger waves were made by combing wet hair flat, applying setting lotion, and creating a series of ridges.

Pin curls were even easier. A woman simply wrapped a small piece of hair around her finger and then secured it with a bobby pin or two. Curls were pinned tightly to the head until they dried.

Make It Permanent

Women with straight hair could spend hours heating curling irons over a flame, or they could sleep with pin curls. Then came the permanent wave. Available at beauty salons, there were two types. One used an electric permanent wave machine, which generated heat. The other was called a "cold wave" and used chemicals, specifically ammonia.

Unfortunately, the processes were still in the early stages. The chemicals and heat caused hair to break. Some scalps were burnt. The results did not always turn out as expected. Still it was the start of the permanents that we enjoy today.

Bleach and Tint

The blonde bombshell was well known in Hollywood. This inspired ordinary women to copy the look. Some women used peroxide or laundry bleach on their own hair.

Hairstyles

Pin curls are elegant and easy to do! You may want to try this retro look for a special occasion or just for fun! All you need to do is wrap pieces of damp hair around your finger and bobby pin the curls close to your head until they dry. Remove the pins and brush through the curls gently to soften the look. You can add a hair clip or maybe even just a plain bobby pin to the side, like the woman in this picture, for some extra glamour. Now you are ready to go!

American actress Jean Harlow (1911–1937) was the original blonde bombshell who changed the face of Hollywood with her platinum blonde locks decades before Marilyn Monroe. Here she is styling her own hair in finger waves!

Hairstyles

It was not that much different in a salon. Bleaching was done with peroxide, ammonia, and soap flakes. It was harsh and burned the scalp. Early colors also were not totally effective. They did not last long. They also did not turn the same color on different women's hair. Plus, they did not always look natural.

But then, in the 1930s, a French company developed a coloring system that stripped the natural color and then added the new color. That was the beginning of bleaching and coloring as we know it today.

Pin It Up

Chignon is a French word that refers to a bun done low at the neck. It requires some hair, and so it was not for the short hairstyles of the 1920s. But a decade later, as women were growing their hair, they were able to wear the chignon.

The chignon was a popular evening look. Hair was pulled back smoothly to show off the face.

Chapter 2

Women's Styles and Fashion

The 1930s was a serious time. People struggled just to survive. After all, this was the Great Depression.

You might think that people would give up on fashion. But they did not. Americans still followed the latest styles. Then they did what they could to change the clothes in their closets if they did not have the money to buy new ones.

Styles were very different from the 1920s. It was noticeable if you were wearing an old dress. In the 1930s, fashion went back to basics. Hemlines were longer, and waistlines were natural. The boyish look was gone. The womanly curve was back.

You could see it in the women's business suits of the day. The suits came in at the waist. Belted jackets were popular. Necklines were cut in a deep "V" to show off blouses. Skirts were long and straight or flared but very feminine.

Evening wear was inspired by Greek drapery. The new styles created elegant floor-length gowns with folds and folds of fabric. It also was a very feminine look.

Bathing suits showed off women's curves. A lot of skin was bared. It was the beginning of the modern look in swimwear.

British actress Madeleine Carroll (1906–1987) poses in a business suit typical of the era, featuring a V-shaped neckline, narrow waist, and hip-hugging skirt. The look is powerful yet feminine. Her peach scarf, gloves, purse, and shoes contrast nicely with the dark gray suit.

15

Dropping Down, Down, Down

Short dresses were iconic of the 1920s, but they became a thing of the past. In the 1930s, hemlines dropped and stayed there.

Necklines dropped, too, and to help emphasize a woman's curves, shaped brassieres came into style. Waistlines further played up femininity with a natural waistline for daywear.

But women still had short dresses in their closets. They added a piece of fabric to the bottom. They also added to the cuffs and collar so that it would look like a design and not just a desperate measure!

Early Recycling

Up until the thirties, it was common to wear a different outfit for morning, afternoon, and evening. The very wealthy still could.

But the majority of Americans could not. People could not afford clothing for every season, let alone every time of day. Instead, they reused their clothes. They made them over on home sewing machines. Outfits did double duty, going from day to night.

Greek Goddesses

That does not mean there was no longer evening wear. The rich could still afford it. They enjoyed the designs of Madame Alix Gres and Madeleine Vionnet.

Madame Alix Gres was a sculptor before she became a designer. She loved the flowing robes in Greek sculptures. She worked to create them in her own designs.

Madame Gres made Grecian-style gowns with heavy draperies and folds. She draped fabric over live models. Then she made the pleats by hand and sewed them together. It was time-consuming, painstaking work. It also meant the dresses were expensive.

French designer Madeleine Vionnet also designed in this Grecian style. She created her gowns from one piece of material without any fastenings. She expected her clients to be able to drape the material in the right places.

Bathing Beauties

Body-hugging bathing suits were in style in the 1920s. In the 1930s, bathing suits went further than that, with even less material and more skin showing.

Suits were one piece but cut lower in the neck and higher on the leg. New knitted and elasticized fabrics hugged figures. In some cases, backs were bare, like modern swimsuits. In fact, some swimsuits from the 1930s resembled today's more conservative styles.

Olympic swimmer Esther Williams showed off swimsuit glamour when she became a Hollywood actress. The bathing suit fashions of the 1930s can be seen in her water ballets featured in many movies of the time.

Fabulous Fashions of the 1930s

These three women enjoy a day at the beach in the conservative bathing suits of the 1920s. The swimsuits of the 1930s still resembled this style, but they revealed more skin, especially necklines, legs, and backs.

A Design Sensation!

Elsa Schiaparelli often caused a sensation with her designs. Consider her desk suit. It was decorated with "drawers" for pockets. Her shoe-shaped hat resembled an upside-down high-heeled shoe.

She once created a silk dress painted with flies. She also created themed collections, such as her circus designs, which showed acrobats and prancing ponies.

Schiaparelli was also one of the first designers to use zippers as a decoration. Until then, people tried to hide zippers because they were just fasteners.

Much of Schiaparelli's influence continues today.

A model smiles for the camera covered head to toe in daisies. Elsa Schiaparelli's bold designs paved the way for unusual fashion, like this gown.

Chapter 3

Men's Styles and Fashion

Men still dressed in tailored suits for formal occasions in the 1930s. But for leisure activities, they adopted a more relaxed look.

Formal wear usually meant a dark-colored suit and tie. The suit jacket had broad shoulders and came in at the waist. The effect was a strong, athletic appearance. Double-breasted jackets were particularly popular, but men also wore single-breasted suits. Trousers had pleats and were held up by suspenders. The finishing touch was the hat, either a trilby or fedora.

For a more casual look, men might choose a Palm Beach suit, which was comfortable in warm weather. The suit was

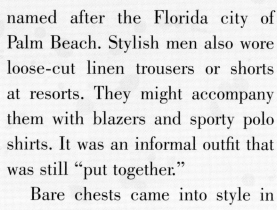

named after the Florida city of Palm Beach. Stylish men also wore loose-cut linen trousers or shorts at resorts. They might accompany them with blazers and sporty polo shirts. It was an informal outfit that was still "put together."

Bare chests came into style in 1934. That was the year of the movie *It Happened One Night*, which inspired many men to skip the undershirts.

When bare chests become acceptable, bathing suits for men, like women, became more body baring. Men wore swim trunks that only covered the bottom half of the body.

A man's double-breasted suit from 1930. Double-breasted meant that it had two columns of buttons on the jacket. In contrast, single-breasted suits only had one column of buttons.

YOU MUST HAVE A PAIR OF SPORTS TROUSERS

For the Good Old Summertime YES! THEY'RE COOL!

Right Up to Date!

You need white twill trousers for tennis, the beach, and all sorts of summer occasions. The slant pockets, wide waist band, set-down belt loops, and 22-inch cuff bottoms are right up to the minute, as are the flaps on the two back pockets. The cotton twill is heavy 8-ounce and PRE-SHRUNK! SIZES—28 to 36 inches waist and 28 to 34 inches inseam. State measurements.

45E7673—High Quality White Twill Trousers. Postpaid............**$1.75**

Flannels Are Style

Style critics agree that plain tan and gray flannel trousers are fast replacing knickers for sport wear. These are of high quality all wool flannel and are cut with the up to date inch pockets and twenty-inch bottoms. Others will ask $6 or $7 a pair for this quality! Sizes—28 to 36 inches waist and 28 to 34 inches inseam. State measurements.

45E7641—Plain Light Tan All Wool Flannel. Postpaid............**$3.98**

45E7642—Plain Light Gray All Wool Flannel. Postpaid............**$3.98**

Genuine Palm Beach

In case of heat—keep cool! You know—Genuine Palm Beach, cool, crisp, comfortable, and washable. The tropical worsteds are over one-third wool, and very light and cool—A hard finished cloth that keeps a crease well. SIZES—30 to 42 inches waist and 29 to 34 inches inseam. State measurements.

45E7563—Medium Dark Gray Striped Genuine Palm Beach. Postpaid............**$3.75**

45E7566—Light Gray Striped Tropical Worsted. Postpaid............**$2.85**

45E7567—Medium Tan Striped Tropical Worsted. Postpaid............**$2.85**

Pre-Shrunk White Duck or Linen

No wonder we lead the field! And now—PRE-SHRUNK! Order the size you need, and it will stay that size no matter how often you wash it! Flaps on two hip pockets. Made just like our regular dress trousers. SIZES—28 to 42 inches waist and 28 to 36 inches inseam. State measurements.

45E7562—Standard Quality White Duck. Postpaid............**$1.19**

45E7565—Higher Quality Heavyweight White Duck. Postpaid............**$1.49**

45E7523—Genuine White Linen. Postpaid............**$2.25**

Stylish Summer Combination
(Sold Separately)

Here is the combination you can't beat for sports wear or for the most dressed up summer occasion! The handsome, well tailored, tan or blue sport jacket is made of fine quality all wool flannel, ¼ lined for coolness. The three patch pockets and the four punch pleats in back give it just the swagger that summer style demands. The trousers are carefully tailored of fine quality all wool white serge with fancy neat black stripes. The stripings are beautiful, and pure worsted means long wear and shape keeping qualities. You can order either of the coats or the trousers separately. SIZES—Coat, 34 to 42 inches chest; Trousers, 28 to 42 inches waist and 28 to 34 inches inseam. State measurements.

45E7320—Medium Light Brown All Wool Flannel Coat. Postpaid............**$9.95**

45E7321—Blue All Wool Flannel Coat. Postpaid............**$9.95**

45E7596—White All Wool Worsted Serge Trousers with Fancy Stripe. Postpaid............

Sport Outfit De Luxe!
(Sold Separately)

Here's a stylish combination of double breasted blue serge coat and plain white flannel trousers. Every man should have at least one such outfit. Now you can save a lot of money. The coat is of excellent quality fine twill blue serge, one-fourth lined, and beautifully tailored—the kind usually sold at $15.00. The trousers are of a standard, nationally known, all wool white flannel, beautifully tailored and really worth $7.50. You can buy either the coat or trousers separately.

SIZES—Coat, Trousers,

Measuring Instructions

This page from a 1931 Sears ® catalog features casual trousers and summer suits. The dark pants at the bottom left are "Genuine Palm Beach." To the right of those are light-colored linen trousers.

It Happened One Night

Movies did a lot to shape men's fashion as well as women's fashion. According to legend, Clark Gable's appearance in *It Happened One Night* was particularly eventful. In a scene with costar Claudette Colbert, Gable took off his shirt to reveal a bare chest.

Men across America took note. If Clark Gable did not have to wear an undershirt, neither did they! If the legend is true, that single movie scene is said to have destroyed the undershirt business overnight.

Perfectly Palm Beach

It was hot in Palm Beach, Florida. That is why the Palm Beach suit was perfect. It was made from light and cool fabric. Examples included cotton seersucker, silk shantung, or linen. It did not matter whether the suit was single-breasted or double-breasted. It was the favorite summer suit of businessmen everywhere.

Blaze to Glory

A blazer is a type of jacket that got its name because it used to be made in blazingly bright colors. University students in England first wore the colored jackets to divide teams playing cricket or tennis.

Blazers soon became popular off campus. Americans wore them in blue, green, brown, and cream colors.

American jazz singer Cab Calloway (1907–1994) dons a zoot suit, a style popular with African Americans in the 1930s. It is characterized by a long blazer with wide padded shoulders and baggy trousers cuffed tightly around the ankles. Sometimes a long watch chain hung from the belt, down the front of the legs, and back to a pocket at the side.

Swim Trunks Take a Dip

Men's bathing suits used to cover their chests. Society prevented men, as well as women, from showing too much skin in a public place like the beach or pool.

But in the early 1930s, that changed. Men started taking off their tops. They did this so often that one designer created a suit where the shirt zipped off.

By 1935, it became commonplace for men to swim without shirts. Once that happened, the trunks changed. Legs were cut higher, and fabrics showed off the body. The modern men's bathing suit had arrived!

Chapter 4
Accessories

During the Depression, accessories became more important than ever. A well-chosen accessory could update fashions quickly. It was much less expensive than an entirely new outfit. The accessories of the 1930s were also more glamorous than the ones from the previous decade. They included jewels, feathers, and furs, for those who could afford them. Women experimented with different kinds of hats, from the exotic fez to the patriotic tricorn, and even the snood, which emerged from a previous era.

Women added belts to evening gowns. The wealthier women accessorized both evening and daytime looks with furs and fur trims. Evening shoes were adorned with gold and silver, but there were more practical shoes for the serious style of the 1930s.

Hats Off to the Fez and Tricorn!

Have you ever seen a fez? This is a brimless hat shaped like a cylinder with a tassel on top. Often made of red felt, the fez was worn, usually by men, in ancient Morocco and other eastern Mediterranean countries. It was also worn by women in the 1930s as a unique accessory. It helped add some pizzazz to an otherwise plain garment that was probably worn for a variety of occasions.

Another dramatic accessory was the tricorn, also spelled tricorne. That is short for tri-corner, or three-corner hat, like those worn during Revolutionary times in the early days of United States. Women accessorized with that hat, too!

Simply Snood

First popular in the 1800s, the snood was brought out again by designer Elsa Schiaparelli in 1935. It also gained popularity when worn in the 1939 hit *Gone With the Wind,* an epic film that was set during the American Civil War and starred Clark Gable and Vivien Leigh.

A snood could almost be described as a hairnet, but it did not go around the entire head. It usually only covered the hair at the back of the head. It was often knitted or crocheted. Sewn into a bag-like shape, it surrounded the hair and was attached at the top. The snood kept hair free from machinery when women worked in factories. It also was a useful accessory for bad-hair days.

This wool snood dangles stylishly from underneath a sheered beaver hat. You could wear the snood by itself or combine it with a hat like this model did.

Fun with Fur

It may seem strange that expensive furs were used in many designs in the 1930s to make or trim clothes. But despite the Great Depression, there were still some wealthy women who could afford them. The furs were used for both day and evening fashions, with flatter furs for day and longer hair for night.

Fur outerwear was also popular. Women wore fur capes over bare shoulders. They wore fur coats. All sorts of furs were used, ranging from sable to mink, chinchilla, and white fox. The most popular furs during the time were silver fox and black monkey.

Fabulous Footwear: Pretty and Practical

There was a new seriousness in shoes in the 1930s. Tailored suits were in fashion, and women needed sophisticated footwear to match. Heels became more businesslike, both lower and broader. That is not to say the shoes were not pretty.

Many Americans were starving during the Great Depression, but some people higher up in the social ladder still had money to spend on fur coats and hats.

SEARS

Sandal

SHOP

$1.98
pair

Ⓐ Sandals are the SHOE OF THE SEASON. We feature "RESORT"—the snow white leather T-strap with cut-out vamp. Leather sole. WOMEN'S SIZES 3½ to 8. C (medium wide) width. State size. Shipping weight. 1 pound
15 L 3207—2½-in. Cuban Heel.
15 L 3208—2-in. Cuban Heel.
Pair $1.98

Ⓑ The support of a Tie with the style of a sandal!! Smooth white leather with cut-out strip across the toe. Flexible leather sole. WOMEN'S SIZES 3½ to 8 C (medium wide) width. State size. Shipping weight. 1 pound
15 L 3209—2½-in. Cuban Heel.
15 L 3210—2-in. Cuban Heel.
Pair $1.98

Ⓒ "BOARDWALK"—the toeless sandal with cut-out heel and perforations. Leather sole. 1¾-inch cuban heel. WOMEN'S SIZES 3½ to 8. C (medium wide) width. State size. Shipping weight, 14 ounces.
15 L 3211—White Leather.
15 L 3212—Chamois Yellow Leather. .... Pair $1.98

Ⓓ "NATIVE"—the charming toeless tie! Belongs under a tropical sun. Leather sole. 1⅞-inch heel. C (medium wide) width. State size. Shipping weight. 15 oz.
15 L 3213—White Leather.
15 L 3214—Blue Leather.
Pair $1.98

Ⓔ "SUN DECK" . . . the pretty T-strap sandal. Beautiful cut-outs. Leather sole. 1¼-inch covered heel. WOMEN'S SIZES 2½ to 8. C (medium wide) width. State size. Shipping weight. 1 lb. 2 oz.
15 L 3235—White Leather.
15 L 3236—Patent Leather.
Pair $1.98

Ⓕ "PROMENADE"—the wide T-strap sandal. Airy cut-outs. Leather sole. 2-inch covered heel. WOMEN'S SIZES 3½ to 8. C (medium wide) width. State size. Shipping weight, 15 oz.
15 L 3215—White Leather.
15 L 3216—Patent Leather.
Pair $1.98

Ⓖ "GRECIAN" sandals inspired by the lovely new flowing styles! Silver kidskin gleams as you dance. One of the most important styles in our Sandal Shop—Sears bring you this $3.00 value for only $1.98! Leather sole. Covered heel. WOMEN'S SIZES 3½ to 8. C (medium wide) width. State size. Shipping weight, 1 pound 1 ounce.
15 L 3153—1¼-Inch Heel.
15 L 3154—2-Inch Spike Heel. Pair $1.98

Sandals became popular as everyday wear in the 1930s. They came open toed, close toed, with T-straps, with laces, and more. Many of the sandals featured here would still be stylish even today!

30

Accessories

The T-strap style of shoe from the 1920s continued its popularity. As the name suggests, the shoe had a strap across the front of the foot and a strap down the middle, forming a *T*. The sling-back shoe, which had a strap that wrapped around the heel of the foot, was an instant hit.

Sandals also became popular for more than the beach. They started to be worn to parties. Eventually, they would be worn as day shoes.

There were evening shoes, too. At first made in silks, satins, and velvets, by the end of the decade, suede was also used. It was popular to pipe on some gold or silver.

Overall, the shoe colors in the 1930s were black, with some maroon, brown, and navy. Brighter colors emerged by the end of the decade.

Chapter 5

Fads and Trends

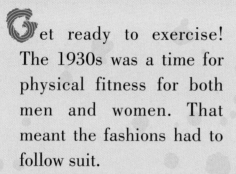

Get ready to exercise! The 1930s was a time for physical fitness for both men and women. That meant the fashions had to follow suit.

Of course, it was not the first time women were exercising. Back in the late nineteenth century, they rode bicycles. Long skirts interfered with the pedaling, and so bicycle suits were allowed.

But the 1930s took sportswear to a higher level. Women did not just have one suit for a sport. They wore shorter, more practical clothes that really allowed them to move!

Going outdoors to exercise was one thing. But another popular pastime was sunbathing. Some sports and leisure clothes featured removable straps so women could get the most from their time in the sun while avoiding awkward tan lines. Bathing suits became lower cut at the front and back. White fabrics were popular to show off a good tan. Sunglasses were all the rage.

About this time, there were also new fabrics available. Science helped create such materials as nylon and metallic lamé. It would be a trend that would last even until today.

Man-made Metallic

Another man-made material became very popular in the 1930s. This was metallic lamé. It was perfect for flashy evening wear and theatrical costumes. The material was made from weaving metallic-colored thread with man-made material. The result was a shimmering gold, silver, bronze, or other metallic shade.

The Birth of Nylon

In the mid-1930s, nylon was invented by researchers at the DuPont Company in Delaware. Nylon was less shiny than rayon. It also fit much better. By the end of the decade, "nylons" had replaced rayon stockings.

They still did not look like the panty hose women wear today. In the thirties, nylon stockings went up until the middle of the thigh. They were held in place by garter belts, stretchy bands that hung down from girdles and clipped onto the tops of the stockings. One-piece panty hose were not invented until much later, in the 1960s.

At the 1939 World's Fair in New York City, the DuPont Company exhibits a machine used to knit nylon stockings. Thigh-high nylon stockings are still in use, but there are also many more styles available to modern women.

Sun Worship

Stylish women used to stay out of the sun because society valued fair complexions. But not in the 1930s. That is when sunbathing became fashionable! Best of all, it did not cost a dime.

Fads and Trends

Famous designer Coco Chanel tanned on the French Riveria. Being tan became associated with the rich. Women loved to show off their tans with the new backless evening gowns of the time. But this love affair with the sun created the need for another accessory—sunglasses.

Before the 1930s, suntans were associated with the working class because many of them worked outdoors. In America especially, where prejudice and discrimination against minorities prevailed, light skin was viewed as the ideal. Then that all changed. Suntanned skin was in. The wealthy had the spare time to lie out in the sun for hours to achieve the look.

FABULOUS FASHIONS of the 1930s

Spending on Sportswear

Physical fitness had become important in America since the late nineteenth century. By the 1930s, beauty was linked with health.

Women were seen playing tennis, archery, and golf. They were fishing, mountaineering, shooting, and skating. Active women needed sportswear so they could move around easily. Designers created tennis dresses with shorts underneath. In 1933, tennis star Alice Marble shocked everyone by wearing shorts without the dress at Wimbledon.

In golf, women wore jackets with skirts, culottes, and even pants. For fishing and shooting, they wore bright wool capes.

Not so different from the modern ideas of beauty, in the 1930s, being physically fit and active was seen as attractive. Tennis was only one of the many sports women played.

Chapter 6

Pop Culture

Life was a struggle during the 1930s. The Great Depression caused many Americans to be out of work. Many wives at the time did not work, so if their husbands lost their jobs, there would be no income at all.

Both men and women did what they could during the Great Depression to find work. Sometimes they worked for food. They grew food in gardens if they could.

They also looked for distractions. If they could not afford to buy books, they went to the library. They played board games. They listened to the radio and went to the movies. Both the radio and the movies were great ways to escape from everyday life.

By 1933, Prohibition was no longer in effect and alcohol was legal. So people went to nightclubs. They danced to swing music, drank, and tried to forget their troubles.

The Great Depression

By the end of the 1920s, there were a lot of people investing in the stock market. The values of companies kept going up, up, up. It seemed like a great way to make money. It was, until October 1929. That is when the stock market crashed. People who invested their life savings lost it all.

That is not all that happened. The banks lost money, too. People became worried. They rushed to withdraw their money. The banks did not have enough. That caused a panic.

At the same time, the economy was weak. Businesses closed. People lost jobs. By 1932, 14 million people were out of work in America. Breadlines and soup kitchens, where people could get free food, were a common sight.

This time period was known as the Great Depression. It would last through most of the decade until World War II helped pull the country out of it.

Radio Rules!

Today, families gather around the television for their favorite programs. That is how it used to be in the 1930s, except families gathered around the radio. Stations broadcast programs from comedies to dramas.

Amos 'n' Andy was the "sitcom" of the 1930s. Listeners followed the adventures of these two. They made plans for a better life, found romance, and so on. The characters were

A family spends quality time together listening to their favorite programs on the radio.

African-American, but due to the societal pressure of the time, the actors who played them were Caucasian.

Radio was also the place for musical programs, where orchestras played and guest stars appeared. President Franklin D. Roosevelt even broadcast his fireside chats over radio, reaching millions of Americans.

During the Great Depression, radio was more than entertainment. It was a comfort to people. It gave them a break from the seriousness of the world.

This woman may be reading a script for a radio drama or reporting the news. Radio was the fastest way entertainment and news could reach millions of people all at once.

Dancing With a Swing

The popular jitterbug was danced to swing music, a bouncy and upbeat type of jazz. Swing crossed racial lines. You could be white, African-American, or Hispanic to play and enjoy swing. Some famous swing musicians included Benny Goodman, Count Basie, and bandleader Cab Calloway.

A movie poster for the 1936 musical *Swing Time* starring Fred Astaire and Ginger Rogers. The dancing duo appeared in ten films together from 1933 to 1949. Their films brought fun and laughter to people's lives during times of hardship.

Movie Musical Mania

The 1930s saw the birth of the movie musical. These were elaborate undertakings, with beautiful costumes and an army of performers.

Director Busby Berkeley was known for his musicals. He would place costumed women in beautiful patterns. Shot from overhead, they would look like a kaleidoscope.

Fred Astaire and Ginger Rogers also appeared in many movie musicals. They were a popular dance team. They tapped and waltzed through many films that remain classic to this day.

Timeline

The 1920s

The look: cloche hats, dropped-waist dresses, long strands of pearls (women), and baggy pants (men)

The hair: short bobs

The fad: raccoon coats

The 1930s

The look: dropped hemlines, natural waists, practical shoes (women), and blazers and trousers (men)

The hair: finger waves and permanents

The fad: sunbathing

The 1940s

The look: shirtwaist dresses and military style (women) and suits and fedoras (men)

The hair: victory rolls and updos

The fad: kangaroo cloaks

The 1950s

The look: circular skirts and saddle shoes (women) and the greaser look (men)

The hair: bouffants and pompadours

The fad: coonskin caps

The 1960s

The look: bell-bottoms and miniskirts (women) and turtlenecks and hipster pants (men)

The hair: beehives and pageboys

The fad: go-go boots

The 1970s

The look: designer jeans (women) and leisure suits (men)

The hair: shags and Afros

The fad: hot pants

The 1980s

The look: preppy (women and men) and *Miami Vice* (men)

The hair: side ponytails and mullets

The fad: ripped off-the-shoulder sweatshirts

The 1990s

The look: low-rise, straight-leg jeans (both women and men)

The hair: the "Rachel" cut from *Friends*

The fad: ripped, acid-washed jeans

The 2000s

The look: leggings and long tunic tops (women) and the sophisticated urban look (men)

The hair: feminine, face-framing cuts (with straight hair dominating over curly)

The fad: organic and bamboo clothing

Glossary

accessories—Items that are not part of your main clothing but worn with it, such as jewelry, gloves, hats, and belts.

blazer—A type of jacket that got its name from the blazing bright colors it used to come in.

chignon—A hair bun wore low at the neck.

double-breasted—A jacket style where one side of the garment overlaps the front of the other side; double-breasted jackets usually have a double row of buttons.

fez—A hat shaped like a cylinder with a tassel on top.

jitterbug—A fast-paced dance performed to swing music, which sometimes involved acrobatics.

lamé—A synthetic material made with metallic-colored thread.

Rhodopane—A glasslike fabric made from cellophane and other synthetic materials.

single-breasted—A style of jacket with a single row of buttons and just a narrow overlap of the two sides when they come together.

snood—A knitted or crocheted baglike hair accessory that surrounds the hair and attaches at the top.

surrealism—An art movement that used fantastical imagery.

tinting—Adding a little bit of color.

trend—The current style or general direction for fashion.

tricorn—A three-cornered hat like the ones worn during America's colonial times.

trousers—An old-fashioned word for men's pants.

undergarments—Garments worn next to the skin and under clothes.

Further Reading

Books

Beker, Jeanne. *Passion for Fashion: Careers in Style.* Toronto, Canada: Tundra Books, 2008.

Costantino, Maria. *Fashions of a Decade: The 1930s.* New York: Facts on File, 2006.

McEvoy, Anne. *The 1920s and 1930s.* New York: Bailey Pub. Associated, 2009.

McKissack, Lisa Beringer. *Women of the Harlem Renaissance.* Minneapolis, Minn.: Compass Point Books, 2007.

Internet Addresses

Fashion-Era, "1930s Fashion History: Stylish Thirties"
<http://www.fashion-era.com/stylish_thirties.htm>

The Costume Gallery, "20th Century Fashion History: 1930s"
<http://www.costumegallery.com/1930.htm>

Index